Pebble™

My World

## In My
# Home

## by Mari C. Schuh

**Consulting Editor:** Gail Saunders-Smith, PhD
**Consultant:** Susan B. Neuman, EdD
Former U.S. Assistant Secretary for Elementary
and Secondary Education
Professor, Educational Studies, University of Michigan

Capstone
press
Mankato, Minnesota

Pebble Books are published by Capstone Press,
151 Good Counsel Drive, P.O. Box 669, Mankato, Minnesota 56002.
www.capstonepress.com

1 2 3 4 5 6 10 09 08 07 06 05

*Library of Congress Cataloging-in-Publication Data*
Schuh, Mari C., 1975–
 In my home / by Mari C. Schuh.
 p. cm. — (Pebble Books. My world)
 Includes bibliographical references and index.
 ISBN 0-7368-4238-1 (hardcover)
 ISBN 0-7368-6116-5 (softcover)
 1. Dwellings—Juvenile literature. 2. Housekeeping—Juvenile literature.
3. Housing—Juvenile literature. I. Title. II. Pebble Books. My world.
(Mankato, Minn.)
TH4811.5.S38 2006
643'.1—dc22            2004029954

Summary: Simple text and photographs introduce basic community concepts related
to homes including location, rooms in a home, and homes around the world.

# Note to Parents and Teachers

The My World set supports national social standards related to
community. This book describes and illustrates homes. The images
support early readers in understanding the text. The repetition of
words and phrases helps early readers learn new words. This book
also introduces early readers to subject-specific vocabulary words,
which are defined in the Glossary section. Early readers may need
assistance to read some words and to use the Table of Contents,
Glossary, Read More, Internet Sites, and Index sections of the book.

# Table of Contents

# My Home

I live in my home
with my family.
Our home keeps us
safe and warm.

My home is on a street.
I play with friends
who live on my street.
We throw snowballs.

My home is
in my neighborhood.
My school is
in my neighborhood too.
I walk to school
from my home.

# Rooms in My Home

My home has
many rooms.
My dad and I
eat in the kitchen.

I rest in my bedroom.

# Other Homes

Families live
in all kinds of homes.
Some homes are big.
Some homes are small.

Some people live in apartments.
Some people live in mobile homes.

Homes are different around the world. In some places, people live in cabins or huts.

I live in a white house.
What kind of home
do you live in?

# Glossary

**apartment**—a building divided into rooms where many people live

**cabin**—a small simple house, often made of wood

**hut**—a small basic house

**mobile home**—a small home that can be moved by pulling it behind a big truck

**neighborhood**—a small area in a town or city where people live

**street**—a road in a city or town, often with sidewalks, houses, or other buildings alongside it

# Read More

**Canizares, Susan and Samantha Berger**. *At Home.* Scholastic Placebook. New York: Scholastic, 2000.

**Chapman, Cindy**. *Where Is Your Home?* Compass Point Phonics Readers. Minneapolis: Compass Point Books, 2004.

**Hill, Lee Sullivan**. *Homes Keep Us Warm.* A Building Block Book. Minneapolis: Carolrhoda Books, 2001.

# Internet Sites

FactHound offers a safe, fun way to find Internet sites related to this book. All of the sites on FactHound have been researched by our staff.

Here's how:

1. Visit *www.facthound.com*

2. Type in this special code **0736842381** for age-appropriate sites. Or enter a search word related to this book for a more general search.

3. Click on the **Fetch It** button.

FactHound will fetch the best sites for you!

# Index

Word Count: 126
Grade: 1
Early-Intervention Level: 10

**Editorial Credits**

Heather Adamson, editor; Juliette Peters, designer and illustrator; Jo Miller, photo researcher; Scott Thoms, photo editor

**Photo Credits**

Capstone Press/Karon Dubke, cover, 1, 4, 6 (all), 8 (all), 10, 12, 16 (bottom), 20 (all)
Folio, Inc./Alan Goldstein, 14 (top)
Houserstock/Dave G. Houser, 18
James P. Rowan, 14 (bottom), 16 (top)

The author dedicates this book to her parents, Mona and Dan Schuh, and to her brothers, Ryan and John Schuh.